Short Stack Editions | Volume 13

by Alison Roman

Short Stack Editions

Publisher: Nick Fauchald
Creative Director: Rotem Raffe
Editor: Kaitlyn Goalen
Copy Editor: Abby Tannenbaum
Wholesale Manager: Erin Fritch

ISBN 978-0-9907853-2-3

Printed in Virginia
Third printing, January 2017

Table of Contents

Drinks

Condiments

Savory

Sweet

You know a recipe is good when it teaches you something new about an ingredient or a method, something that you begin to implement in other ways with other dishes. In these recipes, instructions are more than paint-by-numbers; instead, they build up the confidence and understanding necessary to cook off-book.

These are the types of recipes that Alison Roman has created for lemons. Each is as unfussy and unassuming as lemons themselves, punctuated with Alison's witty, saucy voice. But as we cooked through this book, we were struck by the discoveries hidden between the lines, and the gracefulness of the approach.

The most obvious example is Alison's resolute love of using whole lemons, which figure into everything from lemonade to shaker pie. Her proselytizing has rubbed off on us, and where we once might have just squeezed juice over a pan of just-roasted vegetables, we're now adding lemon wedges to the pan before cooking so they can join in the caramelization fun, as Alison does in her paprika-roasted potatoes on page 27. And after giving the whole-lemon salsa verde (page 19) a spin, we later tried a variation with whole lime to complement a Thai dish—with exceedingly exciting results.

We're better cooks for having followed Alison's recipes, and that, to us at least, is the pinnacle of a cookbook's success. We hope you find this edition equally rewarding.

—*The Editors*

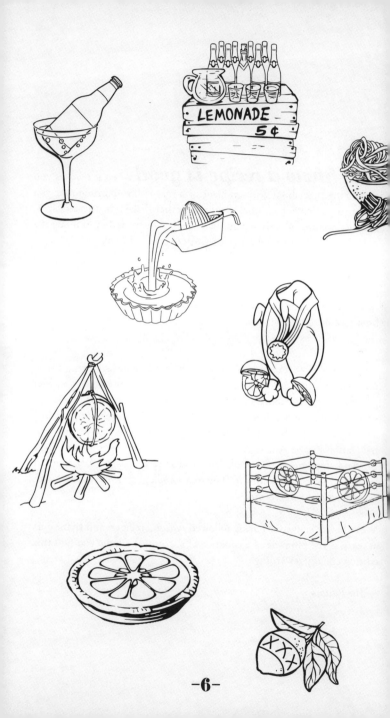

Introduction

Someone once asked me, "If there was one ingredient you could never, ever cook with out, what would it be? And you can't say salt." The choice was obvious, because I've played this game before, and the answer is always the same: lemon. So when I was asked what ingredient I'd like to take on for a Short Stack, it took me all of 5 seconds to decide. To me, a lemon is the single most interesting, versatile, beautiful and delicious thing you can cook with. Sound dramatic? Well, so am I. And so are lemons! Their trademark sourness and bitterness is extreme, and can't be replaced or mimicked (sorry, limes).

My appreciation for lemons dates back many years to when I was small, and started in the most basic of ways: As a kid, I wouldn't drink water unless it had a lemon in it (still won't). Over the years, the desired garnish has grown into a pure, full-blown lemon obsession; I've now gotten to the point where I rarely cook anything without a squeeze, zest or slice of the fruit thrown into it.

Though impossibly easy to find year-round, lemons do, in fact, have a season, although you wouldn't know it in most places. Don't get me wrong: I love New York, but I'm from Southern California, the land of agreeable weather and avocados and juice bars and, yes, citrus. Walking around the farmers' markets during the California "winter" is a magical experience, and not just because it's 73 degrees and sunny.

It's the citrus. Oh, the citrus! The lemons in particular always get me.

Slightly knobbier with coarser skin than the typical grocery store variety, they smell so much like "lemon" that it's almost synthetic, like someone's polishing furniture nearby. I mean that in the way a really ripe strawberry smells like strawberry Chap Stick: so good and pure that you'd swear it was fake. There's just something very delightful about the most sunshine-y fruit being in season during the coldest, produce-starved months. The reality, though, is that a lemon in February and a lemon in July taste pretty much the same, which is great news. They aren't as seasonally sensitive as most produce, which means that you can make many of these recipes whenever, wherever.

I know it's super-Brooklyn of me to be very "whole animal, whole vegetable," etc., but I'm about to get all "whole lemon" on you. Given how ubiquitous and widely used the lemon is, I'm always shocked that so few people use the entire thing. I see just as much virtue in the pith as I do in the zest, and the juice is as valuable as the rind. I'm assuming I love using the whole thing for the same reason I love Campari: Bitterness is a taste we are meant to, well, taste—just as with sharp sourness, which is great complement to all that is fatty, spicy and sweet.

We live in a world where lemons, in my opinion, just don't get the love they deserve. In the wrong hands, a lemon becomes the curly parsley of the fruit world, relegated to garnish, a slice in that vodka tonic or a wedge alongside something fried (which, OK, you need). Let's change that, shall we? Let's not treat lemons as an afterthought, but as a deliberate way to deliver complexity, acidity, bitterness, brightness and, occasionally, sweetness (looking at you, Meyer lemon) to our food. Let's roast them 'til they're jammy and bursting with juices, slice them paper-thin for salads and salsas, caramelize and crisp them in a skillet and juice them to get drunk. Let's celebrate you, dear Lemon—yes, that's a Susan Miller reference—and give you your chance to shine.

—*Alison Roman*

Recipes

Juicing Lemons

You can almost always tell how juicy a lemon will be just by giving it a good squeeze. Is it hard as a rock? Then it's probably not so juicy—try again! The amount of lemon juice you'll get per lemon can vary, but most will yield 3 to 4 tablespoons each.

There are myriad devices and tools to help you juice a lemon, from an electronic juicer to one of those press things they like to use behind the bar. However, in all honesty, I rarely use anything but my hands.* The seeds? I fish or strain them out. But if I'm a fan of any one device, it's those wooden citrus reamers because I find them nice to look at in addition to being helpful (and extremely durable).

*I do own multiple weird citrus presses and reamers and glass juicers and everything else because I am a collector-hoarder of vintage goods, but they are purely ornamental.

Whole Lemonade

The idea for this drink came from a co-worker, Stacey Rivera. Before she could even finish explaining what it was, I heard the words "whole lemonade" and decided it was my new favorite beverage. In her recipe, Stacey actually puts everything together in a blender, which is truly next level. Perhaps this should be called the beginner's version.

2 lemons, scrubbed and sliced   ½ cup sugar
about ¼-inch thick

Muddle the lemons and sugar together using a muddler, rolling pin, wooden spoon or…you get the idea. Muddle until the lemons are pretty broken down; you want to make sure the rind is bruised and the juices are flowing freely. Muddling also helps the sugar dissolve so you don't have to mess around with making simple syrup. Pour 4 cups of water over the lemon-sugar mixture and stir to combine.

If you like, you can turn this into a cocktail by adding some vodka or gin and sipping it over ice. No pressure, though.

Ginger Shandy

I'm not a huge beer drinker, but I am a beer cocktail person. Equal parts beer and lemonade is the kind of beverage that will get you through all your summer barbecues without being the drunkest person there. The ginger is optional, but plenty of ice is not.

---

1 cup Whole Lemonade (page 12) or some other lemonade

2 teaspoons freshly grated ginger

One 12-ounce bottle or can of hefeweizen or light wheat beer

Lemon wedges or wheels, for garnish

serves
·2·

In a pitcher, stir the lemonade and ginger together. Add lots of ice, divide between two glasses and top with beer. Garnish with the lemon wedges. Drink. Repeat.

Meyer Lemon Moonshine

This is one of the easiest things you can do with lemons, and of course the most fun (because it will get you very drunk). Make a ton of it, give it away to friends, keep it for yourself, make a punch with it, whatever. The nice thing about this recipe is that you can make it with other citrus, too—but this book is titled *Lemons* not *Other Citrus*, so that's what I'm sticking with.

Combine strips of zest from about 10 lemons and a 750ml bottle of moonshine (or any other neutral spirit, like vodka) in a large jar and let them mingle for a few weeks. The longer the mixture sits, the more flavorful the 'shine will be.

From here, you can add some simple syrup and bottle it (hello, birthday gifts!) or just keep it around for sipping on ice.

Rosé
All Day

I know, rosé is perfect as it is, so why add anything else? Because cocktail hour, that's why.

1 lemon, thinly sliced

½ cup fresh lemon juice

1 cup Campari or Aperol

¼ cup honey

Dry sparkling rosé wine

Peychaud's bitters

serves
·4·

Combine the lemon, lemon juice, Campari and honey and a few dashes of bitters in pitcher or mixing glass and muddle the lemon slices a bit to break them up. Fill the pitcher with ice and stir to combine. When you're ready to serve, pour into four tall glasses, filling each about ⅓ of the way (make sure you get some lemon slices in each glass. Top each drink with sparkling rosé and more ice, if needed, and serve.

Spicy Preserved Lemons

These salty, tangy, fiery lemons should be in your refrigerator at all times. If you're not familiar with the flavor of preserved lemons, it's sort of like a lemon pickle. They often appear in meat-heavy Middle Eastern recipes as something to cut through all the fat, but I find myself using them for anything that needs a little *je ne sais quoi* (which I translate as "a complex, acidic, bittersweet, floral note").

Many recipes will tell you to use only the rind when cooking with preserved lemons, but you know what? I like to use the whole damn thing. Yes, this recipe yields a lot, but it doesn't really make sense to make a small batch, since preserved lemons keep indefinitely and you'll find endless uses for them. I like mine spicy (because I like just about everything spicy), but feel free to omit the chile if that's more your speed.

8 lemons, scrubbed

1 cup kosher salt

½ cup sugar

10 chiles de arbol, crushed

2 tablespoons black peppercorns, lightly crushed

Boil the lemons in a large pot of water until tender, about 10 minutes. Let cool, then pierce them all over with a paring knife (doing this helps penetrate the inside with brine, so really get in there). Transfer the lemons to a large Mason jar (or divide between two smaller jars).

In a large bowl or glass measuring cup, whisk together the salt, sugar, chile and peppercorns with 6 cups of hot water until the salt is mostly dissolved. Pour the brine over the lemons and seal. Let the jars sit at room temperature for at least two weeks and up to many months (years, if the jars are processed).

Basic Lemon Vinaigrette

Here, the adjective "basic" is a true compliment. This vinaigrette is the ultimate, the only, the best. Lemon juice has a certain acidity and flavor that vinegars can't compete with (mellow, floral, bright, fresh) and seems to complement pretty much anything you can think of. Mixed greens? Obviously. Spooned over seared fish? Yes, 100 percent. Toss with roasted vegetables, cooked grains... yep, you get the idea. You'll want to just keep a jar of it in the fridge, as it'll become your number one. Simple. Good. Basic.

2 tablespoons fresh lemon juice

1 small shallot, finely chopped

1 teaspoon finely grated lemon zest

Pinch of sugar

Kosher salt and freshly ground black pepper

¼ cup olive oil

Combine the lemon juice, shallot, zest and sugar in a small bowl and season with salt and pepper. Let the mixture sit at for least 10 minutes to slightly pickle the shallot. Whisk in the olive oil or, better yet, shake in a small jar. Keep refrigerated. This could take a spoonful of Dijon mustard if you're in the mood.

Lemon Aioli

Real talk: I grew up hating mayonnaise. I don't know what happened, or when it happened, but sometime in my early 20s I realized that what I actually hated was grocery store mayonnaise, and that aioli was really fucking awesome. I like mine like I prefer pretty much everything—very tart—so you should taste as you go and season with more or less juice depending on your preference. This is the kind of aioli that purists would tell you isn't a true aioli because it doesn't contain garlic. If that bothers you, grate a clove into this and please enjoy.

1 large egg yolk

1 tablespoon fresh lemon juice, plus more if desired

1 teaspoon finely grated lemon zest

½ cup grapeseed oil

½ cup olive oil

Kosher salt and freshly ground black pepper

makes
1
cup

Whisk the egg yolk, lemon juice and lemon zest in a small bowl. Combine the grapeseed and olive oils in a measuring cup. Whisking constantly, slowly drizzle in the oil, drop by drop at first, then in a slow steady stream once the mixture starts to thicken, until the aioli is thickened and smooth. Season the aioli with salt, coarsely ground pepper and more lemon juice, if you like. This aioli is on the thicker side, so if you want to use it as a sauce, thin it with a bit of water.

Whole-Lemon Salsa Verde

This is my favorite condiment, and for good reason. It's got all the hits: tons of herbs, lots of olive oil, salt and, yeah, whole lemon. (The whole thing! Wow!) It's the thing I find myself making most often, for lots of meals, because I've found that it will make anything taste better. A dressing for rice, marinade for roasted chicken, dip for flatbread...I mean, come on. The key to using the whole lemon is removing all the seeds before finely chopping it: That's where most of the bitterness comes from (you'll still get a little from the rind, but that's OK and even good). You can add any mix of herbs you fancy: Use parsley as the lion's share, then switch up the remainder depending on what you're serving the salsa with.

½ lemon, seeds removed, finely chopped

2 scallions, thinly sliced

1 garlic clove, finely grated

¾ cup olive oil

1 cup finely chopped parsley

½ cup finely chopped other herbs, such as cilantro, mint, chives or tarragon (include some, a few, or all)

Kosher salt and freshly ground black pepper

Combine all the ingredients in a medium bowl and season with salt and pepper. Although this will keep in an airtight container in the refrigerator for a few days, the herbs will start to discolor after day two.

Lemon & Vanilla-Bean Marmalade

I can't figure out why lemon marmalade isn't more popular, because it's superior to orange marmalade in almost every way (acidity! balance!). I learned how to make marmalade from two sources: my former boss, William Werner, to whom I owe lots of my knowledge, and the *River Cottage Preserves* cookbook, which I worship. This recipe is a sort of hybrid of the two methods, because I liked so much about both and didn't want to choose. It involves soaking and simmering the lemons, which helps soften the peel, take out some of the bitterness and, most importantly, extract the natural pectin. Meyer lemons and regular lemons both work here.

2½ pounds lemons, scrubbed

1 vanilla bean, split and seeds scraped

1 star anise pod

9 cups sugar (yes, 9 cups!)

½ cup fresh lemon juice

makes **6** *jars*

Using a sharp knife, remove the peel and rind from all the lemons. Thinly slice the rinds lengthwise about ⅛-inch thick and set aside. Slice the flesh crosswise, then remove the seeds (the flesh will break down, so don't worry about the thickness). Place the peels and fruit in a large pot with 8 cups of cold water and let sit overnight (you can keep the pot out at room temperature if you don't have space for it in your fridge).

The next day, bring the lemons and water to a boil in a large saucepan. Lower the heat to medium-low and simmer until the peels are completely tender and the water has reduced by about half, 1 to 1½ hours. Add the vanilla bean, star anise and sugar and continue cooking, stirring occasionally, until the mixture is starting to look, well, jammy (the peel will be completely softened, the fruit totally broken down, and the whole thing will be awesomely shiny), about 1½ to 2 hours.

Remove the vanilla bean and star anise and spoon a little marmalade onto a cold plate and chill for 5 minutes; it should gel without running on the plate. Still runny? Reduce the heat to low and keep cooking, stirring pretty much constantly at this point, since the sugar is more likely to burn during the last few minutes of simmering. Once the marmalade is at an ideal thickness, remove the pan from the heat and stir in the lemon juice. Divide among jars and seal immediately.

This marmalade can be refrigerated for up to six months.

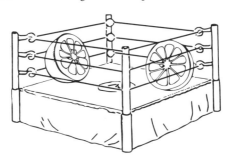

Meyer Lemons vs. Regular

Meyer lemons are the thinner-skinned, slightly sweeter, extremely floral sister of the lemon. While you can absolutely use Meyer lemons in savory applications, they have a pronounced perfume-y flavor, so just use caution when thinking about swapping them with the conventional variety. Also, that supersmooth skin everyone is always praising is REALLY hard to zest, so when a recipe calls for a bunch of zest, I like to stick with regular lemons.

Avocado Toast with Aleppo Pepper & Lemon Relish

It took me a while to appreciate avocados, mostly because I thought they were boring and bland. That was until I started assaulting them with lemon every time I ate one. I like using the whole lemon in lots of places, but here I use only the flesh and the zest because you're eating a lot of it at once. Oh, and this relish is pretty good on most things, so make extra and keep it handy.

1 lemon

1 small shallot, halved through the root and thinly sliced

1 tablespoon finely chopped capers

1 teaspoon Aleppo pepper

4 tablespoons olive oil, divided, plus more for drizzling

Kosher salt and freshly ground black pepper

2 cups arugula or watercress

½ cup parsley, tender stems and leaves

2 tablespoons tarragon leaves

2 avocados—pitted, peeled and quartered

serves ·4·

4 thick slices toast of your choice (something seedy would be good here)

2 tablespoons toasted sunflower or pumpkin seeds

Flaky or coarse sea salt

Using a peeler, remove 4 strips of lemon zest from the lemon. Finely chop the zest and set aside. Using a paring knife, remove the remaining skin and any white pith from the lemon and discard. Discard any seeds, then finely chop the flesh of the lemon. Transfer the lemon and the chopped zest to a small bowl and add the shallot, capers, Aleppo and 2 tablespoons of the oil; season with salt and pepper and let sit for 5 to 10 minutes to let all the flavors meld.

In a large bowl, toss the arugula, parsley and tarragon with the remaining 2 tablespoons of olive oil and season with salt and pepper. Smash the avocado pieces onto the toasts with a fork and top with plenty of relish.

Scatter the salad over the toast, then drizzle with additional olive oil and sprinkle the seeds and some flaky salt on top for good measure.

Beet Salad with Cucumber, Lemon & Pistachios

Yes, you can eat beets raw—and you should. They are crisp, earthy and sweet, but totally in need of some serious acid (thanks, lemon!). It's pretty important to slice the lemons as thinly as possible here (don't worry too much about them keeping their round shape). Use a sharp knife; a mandoline will tear the lemons instead of slicing them. This is the kind of palate cleanser-esque side dish that should be eaten with a large fatty cut of meat that's either roasted or braised.

2 small golden or red beets, peeled and thinly sliced

½ lemon, seeds removed, very thinly sliced

½ small red onion, thinly sliced into rings

¾ teaspoon mild honey

Kosher salt and freshly ground black pepper

2 tablespoons olive oil

2 Persian cucumbers (or half of 1 hothouse cucumber), thinly sliced

2 tablespoons chopped pistachios

¼ cup coarsely chopped cilantro

1 teaspoon nigella seeds or black sesame seeds

serves
-4-

Combine the beets, lemon, onion and honey in a medium bowl. Season with salt and pepper and let sit for at least 20 minutes to soften the beets. Add the olive oil, cucumber, pistachios, cilantro and nigella seeds, tossing to coat. Season with more salt and pepper and more nigella seeds if you like.

Wilted Greens with Crispy Lemon & Chickpeas

I made "crispy lemons" for the first time by accident when I was cooking for some friends ("crispy" being code for "almost burnt"). They turned out to be a total hit, so I started making them on purpose. I now eat some variation of this dish at least once a week. Sometimes I throw a fried egg on it and call it breakfast. Sometimes I come home and make it at 1 a.m. and call it dinner. Whatever I call it, I really can't seem to get enough.

¼ cup olive oil

1 lemon, thinly sliced, seeds removed

2 garlic cloves, smashed

4 chiles de arbol

One 15-ounce can chickpeas—drained, rinsed well and patted dry

One two-inch piece of fresh turmeric, finely chopped (or ⅛ teaspoon ground)

1 large bunch kale or Swiss chard, ends trimmed

Kosher salt and freshly ground black pepper

⅓ cup whole Greek yogurt or labne

¼ cup cilantro, tender leaves and stems

serves
-4-

Heat the oil in a large skillet over medium-high heat. Add the lemon and garlic and swirl to coat. Cook, swirling occasionally to promote even browning, until the lemons are golden brown. Using a slotted spoon, remove the lemon and garlic from the skillet and transfer to a paper-towel-lined plate (the lemons will crisp as they cool).

Return the skillet with the oil to medium-high heat. Add the chickpeas, turmeric and chile de arbol. Cook, swirling occasionally, until the chickpeas are browned and crisped, 8 to 10 minutes (you'll notice the skins start to shrivel up and look almost fried). Using a slotted spoon, transfer the chickpeas and chiles to the plate with the lemons and garlic.

Add the greens to the skillet, tossing with tongs so the greens become coated with oil. Season with salt and pepper and cook until just wilted, about 2 minutes. Return the chickpeas, lemons and garlic to the skillet and toss to coat.

Scoop the yogurt onto a large plate, top with the cooked greens mixture and the cilantro and serve. If you're feeling ambitious, fry up a few eggs and lay them on top; this could even pass for breakfast.

Lemon-Pickled Shrimp with Fennel

I love a pickled shrimp, but often find the ones pickled in vinegar too harsh. Using lemon juice in addition to vinegar creates a milder brine. You can serve these guys in cute little jars at cocktail parties or chop everything up and serve the mixture with fat slices of buttered toast.

½ cup olive oil

6 strips lemon peel

1 teaspoon coriander seed

½ teaspoon fennel seed

1 pound medium shrimp, peeled and deveined

½ cup fresh lemon juice

¼ cup apple cider vinegar (preferably unfiltered)

½ medium bulb fennel, very thinly sliced

¼ yellow onion, very thinly sliced

Kosher salt and freshly ground black pepper

serves -4-

Heat the olive oil, lemon peel and coriander and fennel seeds in a small skillet or saucepan over medium heat until the lemon zest is sizzling and the coriander and fennel start to smell toasty, about 4 minutes. Remove the pan from the heat and let cool completely.

While the oil is cooling, bring a large pot of salted water to a boil. Add the shrimp and cook until bright pink and just cooked through, about 2 minutes. Drain and rinse under cold water.

Once the oil is cool, transfer it to a medium bowl and whisk in the lemon juice and vinegar, then add the fennel, onion and shrimp. Season with salt and pepper and toss to coat. Divide the shrimp mixture among small jars or pour into one large jar. Let them pickle for at least 30 minutes or up to overnight. (They are still good after a few days, but will toughen up slightly as they sit in the brine, so they're best eaten within a day or two.)

Paprika-Roasted Potatoes & Lemon

Roasting lemon wedges gives them a juicy, jammy, caramelized texture that is unsurprisingly perfect with creamy, starchy potatoes. If I were you, I'd double down and serve these with lemon aioli (page 18), but I won't tell you how to live your life.

1½ pounds Yukon Gold potatoes, halved (quartered if large)

1 lemon, cut into 4 wedges, seeds removed

½ small onion, thinly sliced

¼ teaspoon smoked hot paprika

4 sprigs rosemary

¼ cup olive oil

Kosher salt and freshly ground black pepper

serves 4

Preheat the oven to 450°.

Toss the potatoes, lemon, onion, paprika, rosemary and olive oil on a rimmed baking sheet. Season with salt and pepper and roast, tossing everything occasionally, until the potatoes are cooked through, deeply browned and crispy, and the lemons are caramelized and jammy, 35 to 40 minutes. Transfer the mixture to a platter or bowl and squeeze the lemons over the potatoes before serving.

Lemony Pasta with Pecorino & Cracked Pepper

Call me an 8-year old, but I don't think there is anything better than pasta with salt, butter and cheese. However, when you're older, adding lemon and lots of cracked pepper makes it socially acceptable to serve at dinner parties. You're welcome! Although this recipe calls for store-bought pasta for brevity's sake, let me take this moment to say that if you are in the habit of making your own pasta, grate some lemon zest into the dough next time; you'll be so pleased.

1 lemon

4 tablespoons unsalted butter

2 tablespoons olive oil

1½ tablespoons finely grated lemon zest (from about 2 lemons)

1½ teaspoons coarsely ground black pepper

1 teaspoon coarsely ground pink peppercorns, plus more for sprinkling

2 sprigs lemon (or regular) thyme, divided, plus more leaves for sprinkling

10 ounces fettuccine or linguine

Kosher salt

½ cup grated pecorino, plus more for shaving

2 tablespoons finely chopped chives

¼ cup parsley leaves, torn

⅓ cup toasted walnuts, crushed

serves
-4-

Bring a large pot of salted water to a boil.

Quarter the lemon and remove the seeds. Finely chop one quarter and set the rest aside for squeezing over later.

In a large skillet, heat the butter and olive oil over medium heat, then add the chopped lemon, lemon zest, black pepper, pink pepper and 2 thyme sprigs. Cook, swirling the skillet occasionally, until everything is very fragrant and the zest begins to brown a little, a few minutes.

Meanwhile, cook the pasta in the boiling water until tender. Drain, reserving 1 cup of pasta cooking liquid. Add the pasta and ½ cup of the cooking water to the skillet and toss to coat, cooking for a minute or two to thicken the sauce. Add the grated pecorino and keep tossing until a thick, glossy sauce has formed, adding more pasta water as needed to get that sauce going and make it thicker (use tongs; they will make this much faster and easier). Add the chives and the remaining 2 sprigs of thyme and toss to coat.

Divide the pasta among shallow bowls and top with the parsley and walnuts. Serve with shaved pecorino and crushed pink peppercorns for sprinkling, and the remaining lemon wedges for squeezing over the top.

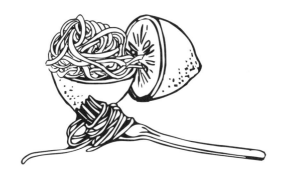

Lemon-Roasted Chicken with Rye Croutons

When I say that I make the best roast chicken, it's at the very least arrogant, and also likely untrue. But just let me have this one, OK? When I found out that the key to great fried chicken was a buttermilk brine, I figured that the same must be true when applied to a whole roasted one. Brining the bird overnight in a buttermilk-lemon bath not only tenderizes the meat, making it juicy beyond your wildest dreams, but the sugars in both the buttermilk and the fruit also help to brown the skin in a way you never thought possible.

1 quart buttermilk

¼ cup fresh lemon juice

2 garlic cloves, finely grated, plus 1 head garlic, halved lengthwise

½ bunch rosemary, chopped

Kosher salt and freshly ground black pepper

One 3½- to 4-pound chicken

4 lemons, 2 halved and 2 thinly sliced, seeds removed

1 large shallot, halved

4 tablespoons unsalted butter, at room temperature

2 cups rye bread, torn into 2-inch pieces

serves
-4-

Whisk the buttermilk, lemon juice, grated garlic, rosemary, 1 tablespoon of salt and 1 teaspoon of pepper in a large bowl or measuring cup. Place the chicken in a large Ziploc bag and pour the buttermilk mixture over it. Seal the bag and shake it, distributing the brine all over the chicken. Let the chicken sit in the refrigerator at least 8 hours, ideally up to 12.

When you're ready to roast the chicken, preheat the oven to 425°. Remove the chicken from the brine and pat dry with paper towels (no need to rinse).

Place the bird on a rimmed baking sheet and stuff the cavity with the 2 halved lemons, shallot, halved head of garlic and sage. Starting at the neck opening of the chicken, loosen the skin from the breast by placing your hands under the skin, reaching all the way down and separating the skin from the meat. Tuck the lemon slices under the skin and on top of the breasts, taking care not to rip the skin (it's pretty resilient, but just be careful). Rub the butter all over the bird and roast until the skin is deeply browned and golden all over, about 30 to 35 minutes.

Reduce the temperature to 375° and add the bread cubes to the roasting pan, tossing to coat them in the pan juices. Continue roasting until the bread is browned and crusty and an instant-read thermometer inserted into the deepest part of the chicken thigh reaches 165°, about 25 to 30 minutes longer. Because of the aforementioned sugars, the chicken may start to brown too much before it's cooked through; if that happens, you can tent the bird with some foil to protect it from burning.

Remove the chicken from the oven and let it rest at least 10 minutes before carving and serving with the croutons.

Clams in Lemon Broth

I'd say most foods are enhanced by lemon, but few foods *must* be eaten with lemon. Clams are one of those foods. Look for the cute, tiny littleneck clams if you can find them.

2 tablespoons unsalted butter

2 tablespoons olive oil

4 garlic cloves, thinly sliced

2 lemons, zested and juiced

4 pounds littleneck clams, scrubbed

½ cup dry white wine (such as Sauvignon Blanc or something similar)

2 tablespoons chopped parsley

1 tablespoon chopped dill

Crusty bread, for serving

serves ·4·

Heat the butter and olive oil in a large Dutch oven (or your largest pot) over medium-high heat. Add the garlic and lemon zest and cook, stirring occasionally, until the garlic and zest are soft and fragrant but not browned, about 2 minutes.

Add the clams and white wine, stirring to coat the clams with the other ingredients. Cook until most of the wine has evaporated, about 2 minutes. Add the lemon juice and ¾ cup of water and cover the pot. Cook until the clams are starting to open, anywhere from 3 to 5 minutes. Sprinkle with parsley and dill and serve in a big old bowl with some crusty bread for sopping up all those juices.

Mackerel in Chile Oil with Lemon & Scallion

Fatty, oily fish has a special fondness for lemon. Here, the lemons kind of melt into the oil as you slow-roast the fish, rendering them totally tender and delicious. If you haven't quite hopped aboard the mackerel train, salmon or cod would also be great here.

1½ pounds mackerel fillets (or 1½ pounds skinless salmon or cod fillets)

Kosher salt and freshly ground black pepper

1½ cups olive oil

2 teaspoons crushed red chile flakes

2 star anise pods

1 teaspoon cumin seeds

1 lemon, thinly sliced, seeds removed

4 scallions, thinly sliced on the bias

2 celery stalks, thinly sliced on the bias

serves
—4—

Preheat the oven to 300°. Season the fish fillets with salt and pepper and place, skin side down, in a medium baking dish (they should be snug, but not overlapping). Heat the oil in a medium skillet over medium heat. Add the chile flakes, star anise, cumin and lemon and cook for a few minutes, swirling the skillet occasionally to let everything mingle. Once the spices are fragrant and the lemon slices begin to sizzle, remove the mixture from the heat and pour over the mackerel.

Place the mackerel in the oven and roast until the fish is just cooked through, about 20 minutes. Once the fish is done, transfer it to a large serving platter (or divide among several individual plates) and top with scallion and celery. Spoon the chile oil, as well as any lemon slices left in the baking pan, over the fillets and serve.

Butcher's Steak with Charred Lemon & Garlic Butter

Yes, there is steak, but let the lesson here be about the charred lemon. When you cook a lemon over high heat, cut side down, some wonderful things happen. The sugars caramelize, the juices flow, the flavor mellows. I've gotten into the habit of throwing some lemons down into the skillet (or on the grill) whenever I'm making chicken or steak to serve alongside for squeezing over. Even better, chop up that charred lemon to throw into some garlic butter.

4 tablespoons unsalted butter, softened	Kosher salt and freshly ground black pepper
2 garlic cloves, finely grated	2 tablespoons vegetable oil
2 anchovy fillets, finely chopped (optional)	1 lemon, quartered
1 tablespoon finely chopped parsley, plus more	1½ pounds hanger steak, halved (about one large steak)

serves
-4-

In a small bowl, smash the butter with the garlic, anchovy and 1 table-spoon of parsley. Season with salt and pepper and set aside.

Heat 1 tablespoon of the oil in a medium skillet over medium-high heat. Sear the lemon quarters, cut side down, until caramelized; using tongs, turn the lemons and continue to sear until they are lightly charred all over, about 4 minutes. Remove the lemons from the skillet and set aside to cool.

Wipe the skillet clean and heat the remaining 1 tablespoon of oil over medium-high heat. Season the steak with salt and pepper and sear until the steak is deeply browned on both sides, about 4 minutes per side. Transfer the steak to a cutting board and let rest at least 5 minutes.

While the meat rests, remove the seeds from one of the lemon quarters, then finely chop it. Add that (and any of the juices that have escaped during chopping) to the garlic butter; season it again with salt and pepper, if necessary. Slice the steak against the grain into 1-inch-thick pieces. Transfer the meat to plates and spoon the butter on top, letting it melt between slices. Sprinkle with parsley and serve with the remaining charred lemon quarters for squeezing over.

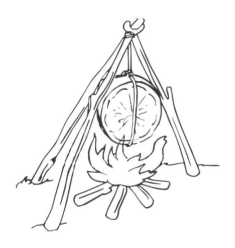

Lemon Tart with Whipped Ricotta

This tart is basically an excuse to eat lemon curd with cheese, which are two of life's greatest things. Together, even better. Finding the perfect lemon curd is a very personal experience, since some prefer it very creamy, others very tart, maybe a bit runny or perhaps the texture of whipped cream. This one has lots of butter and also uses whole eggs, making it pretty thick—and thus ideal for tart filling. I also prefer mine on the tangy side, which some interpret as mouth-puckering, so you can always increase the sugar by up to ¼ cup if you're not a diehard lemon lover (but if you're not, what are you doing reading this?).

For the crust:

1½ cups all-purpose flour

1 tablespoon sugar

Kosher salt

½ cup unsalted butter, chilled, cut into ½-inch cubes

1 large egg, beaten to blend

For the filling:

1 cup fresh lemon or Meyer lemon juice

¾ cup sugar

2 large eggs

4 large egg yolks

¼ teaspoon kosher salt

¾ cup (1½ sticks) unsalted butter, chilled, cut into ½-inch cubes

1 cup whole-milk ricotta cheese

2 tablespoons confectioner's sugar

Flaky or coarse sea salt

makes one **9** IN. tart

Make the crust: Preheat the oven to 350°. Combine the flour, sugar and ¾ teaspoon of salt in a medium bowl. Add the butter and, using your hands or a pastry cutter, rub the butter into the dry mixture until it's pretty well incorporated. Using a fork, add the egg and 2 tablespoons of

ice water and mix until a shaggy dough forms, kneading it all together to incorporate any dry spots. Form into a disc, wrap tightly in plastic wrap and refrigerate until the dough is pretty firm, about 2 hours.

On a lightly floured work surface, roll the dough out into an 11-inch round. Press the dough into a 9-inch tart pan. Line the dough with parchment paper and fill it with baking beans or rice. Bake until the crust is light golden brown, 10 to 12 minutes. Remove the baking beans and continue to bake until the crust is totally baked through and golden brown, another 10 to 12 minutes. Let cool completely.

Make the filling: Whisk the lemon juice, sugar, eggs, yolks and salt in a medium saucepan. Place over medium heat and cook, whisking constantly (to prevent scrambled eggs), until the mixture has thickened, about 5 minutes. Remove the mixture from the heat and transfer to a blender. With the blender on low speed, slowly add the butter, a few pieces at a time (this creates the silkiest, smoothest curd ever). Once the butter has been totally incorporated, pour the curd into the tart shell and refrigerate for at least 3 hours.

To serve, whip the ricotta and powdered sugar together in a large bowl until supersmooth and creamy (just a bowl and a whisk will do here). Smear the mixture on top of the lemon curd, then sprinkle all over with the flaky salt.

Lemon Shaker Pie

This is, hands down, my favorite pie. I make it in the winter because there isn't a ton of other fruit around, and then I keep making it all year long because it's just the best. Letting the sliced lemons sit overnight in sugar softens them before baking, so they get all melty and jammy in the oven.

For the crust:

Double the crust recipe for the Lemon Tart with Whipped Ricotta (page 36) and use that!

makes
one
9 IN.
pie

For the filling:

2 Meyer lemons, very thinly sliced, seeds removed

1¼ cup sugar, plus more for sprinkling

Kosher salt

4 large eggs, divided

¼ cup all-purpose flour

2 tablespoons unsalted butter, at room temperature

Reserve a few lemon slices to put on top of the pie and combine the rest with the sugar and ¼ teaspoon of salt in a medium bowl. Toss to coat, then refrigerate for at least 8 hours and up to 24 hours.

Preheat the oven to 350°. Roll out one piece of dough into an 11-inch round and transfer to a 9-inch pie dish (not deep dish!), leaving all of the overhang. Roll out the second piece of dough into an 11-inch round and chill.

Remove the lemons from the refrigerator and whisk in 3 of the eggs and flour. Stir in the butter and pour the mixture into the crust.

Remove the second round of dough from the refrigerator, cut in vents or circles or whatever clever pie design you desire and then drape it over the pie filling. Press the top and bottom crusts together, creating a seal. Using a knife or scissors, trim the overhang, leaving about 1 inch all around. Using the tines of a fork, press the crusts together to seal completely and create an awesome pattern.

In a small bowl, beat the remaining egg with a fork. Brush the egg wash all over the pie and arrange the reserved lemon slices on top. Sprinkle the whole thing with sugar and bake until the crust is deeply golden and evenly browned, 70 to 80 minutes.

Let the pie cool at least 2 hours before serving: this may be one of the few pies that tastes better at room temperature, even chilled.

Coconut-Lemon Tea Cake

This is the kind of cake you can throw together when someone calls you and says "We're having a party tonight, want to come? Bring dessert!" and you think to yourself, "Oh shit! I don't have time/ingredients/equipment to make anything!" Relax. You've got this. Rubbing the sugar and zest together is not just an annoying step bakers tell you to do to complicate your life; it really does infuse the sugar with lemon flavor, which will go a long way here.

Nonstick vegetable oil spray

1½ cups all-purpose flour, plus more for dusting

2 teaspoons baking powder

Kosher salt

1¼ cup sugar, divided

2 tablespoons finely grated lemon zest

¾ cup whole-milk Greek yogurt

½ cup melted coconut oil (or vegetable oil)

2 large eggs

½ cup unsweetened coconut flakes

2 tablespoons fresh lemon juice

makes 1 loaf

Preheat the oven to 350°. Coat a loaf pan lightly with vegetable oil spray and line with parchment paper (go ahead, spray that too).

In a medium bowl, whisk the flour, baking powder and ¾ teaspoon of salt and set aside. Using your fingers, rub 1 cup of the sugar with the lemon zest in a large bowl until the sugar is fragrant and yellow and smells just like you rubbed a lemon in there. Whisk in the yogurt, coconut oil and eggs. Add the flour mixture and whisk just to blend.

Pour the batter into your prepared pan and smooth the top. Sprinkle coconut flakes over the surface and bake until the top of the cake is golden brown, the edges pull away from the side of the pan and a tester inserted into the center comes out clean, 50 to 55 minutes.

While the cake bakes, combine the lemon juice and remaining ¼ cup of sugar in a small saucepan and bring it to a simmer; cook until the sugar has dissolved. Turn off the heat and keep the mixture warm. When the cake comes out of the oven, brush the top with the syrup, then return the cake to the oven and bake for 5 minutes longer to recrisp the coconut. Remove the cake and let it cool completely before serving.

Lemon Verbena Shortbread Cookies

File this recipe under "make a double batch," because these cookies will disappear very, very quickly. This dough is pretty versatile, and you can do a lot with it. Roll it into logs for slice-and-bake action or roll it out to cut out into cute little shapes. The choice is yours. Choose your own adventure!

1 cup (2 sticks) chilled unsalted butter, cut into ½-inch pieces	1 tablespoon finely chopped lemon verbena (or lemon thyme if you can't find it)
½ cup granulated sugar, plus more for sprinkling	Kosher salt
¼ cup powdered sugar	2½ cups all-purpose flour
	1 large egg, beaten to blend

makes 20 cookies

Preheat the oven to 350°. Using an electric mixer on medium-high speed, beat the butter, granulated sugar, powdered sugar, verbena and ½ teaspoon of salt until very light and fluffy, 7 to 10 minutes (yes, that's a long time– but worth it for superflaky, tender shortbread). Reduce the speed to low and add the flour, mixing just to combine—don't overmix or your cookies will be tough.

Now that you've made the dough, you can either roll it up in parchment paper into logs to chill and slice into ½-inch rounds, or roll the dough ½-inch thick and cut out little rectangles or circles. Either way, brush the tops with some of the egg and sprinkle with some granulated sugar. Bake until the shortbread is golden brown, 10 to 12 minutes. Let cool on a rack before eating. The cookies can be stored in an airtight container for up to 1 week; the dough can be frozen for up to 1 month.

Meyer Lemon & Saffron Sorbet

When I was little, my mom would buy these little Italian ice cups from Costco, and the lemon ones were always the first to go (because I ate them all). This is my homage to them. I guess that technically this is a sherbet because it contains dairy, but to be honest, I can't stand that word, so let's stick with sorbet.

Generous pinch of good quality saffron threads

1 cup sugar

¾ cup fresh Meyer lemon juice

1 tablespoon finely grated lemon zest

¾ cup whole-milk Greek yogurt

In a small saucepan, simmer the saffron with ½ cup of water until the saffron has bloomed, about 2 minutes. Whisk in the sugar to dissolve and let cool completely. Whisk in the lemon juice, lemon zest and yogurt and freeze in your ice cream maker if you have one. If you don't, I guess you could just drink this. I probably would.

Thank You!

Thanks, of course, to Nick and Kaitlyn for being so patient with me and the delivery of this manuscript, but also for giving me this opportunity/soapbox in the first place. I think what you guys are doing is revolutionary and also completely inspiring. I'm so, so happy to be a part of it.

Thank you to my work family at *Bon Appetit* for teaching me how to be a better cook, editor, writer, eater and drinker. To my actual family, for always being so proud of me, even though Mom, when I first told you I was going to give working in a restaurant a try, you were afraid that meant I would end up working at Hot Dog on a Stick (in the mall!). To my friends and Honeypots for always being hungry and volunteering to do the dishes (you all clean better than I do, anyway). To Jen and James for letting me micro-manage Sunday Family Dinner and destroy your kitchen every week. To every boss and mentor I've ever had for knowing I could do something before I did (and not firing me when maybe I couldn't).

—Alison Roman

Share your Short Stack cooking experiences with us
(or just keep in touch) via:

#shortstackeds   facebook.com/shortstackeditions

@shortstackeds   hello@shortstackeditions.com

Colophon

This edition of Short Stack was printed by Stephen Gould Corp. in Richmond, Virginia on Neenah Astrobrights Lift-Off Lemon (interior) and Neenah Oxford White (cover) paper. The main text of the book is set in Futura and Jensen Pro, and the headlines are set in Lobster.

Available now at *ShortStackEditions.com:*